Dee Johnson

SPELLS
for
PROSPERITY

First published in Great Britain in 2024 by

Greenfinch
An imprint of Quercus Editions Ltd
Carmelite House
50 Victoria Embankment
London EC4Y 0DZ

An Hachette UK company

A CIP catalogue record for this book is available from the British Library

HB ISBN 978-1-52943-899-4
Ebook ISBN 978-1-52943-900-7

10 9 8 7 6 5 4 3 2 1

Design by Sooky Choi
Cover design and illustrations by Holly Ovenden

Printed and bound in Great Britain by Clays Ltd, Elcograf S.p.A.

Papers used by Greenfinch are from well-managed forests and other responsible sources.

Dee Johnson

SPELLS
for
PROSPERITY

*Enchantments for Wealth,
Luck and Success*

greenfinch

CONTENTS

INTRODUCTION

Welcome to the enchanting realm of prosperity spells, a magickal and mystickal journey revealing the secrets of creating money, abundance and success for yourself. These spells have been created for both a beginner and an advanced practitioner of the arts, and are particularly suited to those wishing to manifest positive energy and to attract prosperity into their lives. There is a spell here for everyone.

Many of us have been trained to believe that expressing a desire to have money means we are greedy, however without money we don't have stability in our lives. Having financial security creates a life without worry and enables us to live happy and fulfilled lives. With all the money we need and some extra, we also have the option to donate to charity.

MANIFESTING WEALTH

Money is essential to owning or renting a home, buying food and keeping your loved ones feeling secure. It does not buy happiness, however it does offer stability and comfort, so creating a more fulfilling and happier life.

In today's fast-paced, competitive world, people seek different ways to attract wealth into their lives. This book shows you different ways in which to create money – from doubling your money spells to business success spells and fast money spells. Long known for their ancient wisdom and mysterious powers, prosperity spells can manifest financial wealth and attract opportunities by aligning with the unlimited abundance that the universe gifts us.

Deeply rooted in mystickal and magickal traditions, prosperity spells use focused intentions, visualization and observation of the moon phases and planetary aspects to enhance financial growth and overall wealth. Working with the universal forces of abundance, these spells can bring about positive changes as well as creating opportunities for success.

Within the following pages, you'll discover a sparkling selection of spells, each specially crafted to create prosperity and abundance. Each one tells you the best time to cast the spell and includes step-by-step instructions for you to follow. From the glow of candlelight to the scent of mystical herbs, these spells invite you to cast them in a magickal celebration of intention and manifestation.

These enchanting spells have been used to bring success and positive changes to many people's lives. Harnessing the power of the universe combined with esoteric wisdom, they have the potential to manifest your wildest dreams. Whether you believe in magick or not, it's important to cast these spells with utter confidence to achieve your financial goals and create a prosperous life for yourself and your loved ones. Unleash your inner power and turn your dreams into reality.

CASTING A SPELL

Casting spells is an art and practice makes perfect. It can be a powerful and enlightening experience. The more spells you cast, the more confident you will feel. Witches believe in the power of spells and use them as a personal means of empowerment. You, too, can have this power. Words and thoughts hold much power – you need to believe in the magick of your spells for them to come true.

Before casting a spell, witches raise their vibration, or energy. This can be done through dance, meditation or by listening to your favourite music. Anything that 'lifts' you is a good choice. . .you are literally charging yourself up to push your spell up and out into the universe. Visualization is popular with witches: visualize a sparkling gold light flowing from the sky and into your head, right down through your body, and flowing out from your feet.

Witches are often work (skyclad) when working with magick. This is a personal choice. If you prefer, you could wear a special dress or cloak. Be mindful to wrap up warm if you choose to cast your spell outside and it's a cold night. You don't want to be feeling uncomfortable in the middle of your spell-casting.

Casting spells requires preparation and a positive approach in order to ignite whichever spell you are performing. Organization is key. When you have worked out the best time to cast your spell, become excited about it. Liken it to a date in your diary, a special night out. This starts to build up energy. Every time you think about the event, you are adding power for a favourable outcome. Consider taking the day off work or cancelling any prior engagements to ensure that you are in a positive mind frame on the day.

Before casting a spell, make sure you will not be interrupted. Turn off your phone, set the scene, light naturally scented candles and dim the lights. Always use a lighter to light candles, and never matches, as the sulphur will kill your spell. Never blow a candle out, but always use a snuffer to extinguish it, otherwise you will blow your spell away.

A ritual bath or shower before casting a spell is important as it cleanses your body of any negative energy you might have picked up during the day. I recommend using a naturally scented bath or shower wash. Your local health food shop will have a good selection.

Spells should come directly from your heart, with positive thoughts only. After a spell has been cast it's really important not to speak about it as this can weaken or break it. Other people's opinions might not align with yours and negative words from a friend could put doubt into your mind, so it's best to avoid this. Keeping your spell to yourself keeps it pure and strong.

INTENSIFY YOUR POWER

To add extra power to a spell, create an energy ball before casting. Place your hands together, palms cupped and slightly parted. Visualize an electric blue ball between your hands. Shape it into an energy ball of power to assist you in your spell work. When you feel ready, gently push the ball into your solar plexus. This will boost your energy for your spell work.

THE WITCH'S STORE CUPBOARD

The spells in this book are simple and easy to follow – perfect for both a beginner and an advanced practitioner of the arts – and have been created using the following accessible tools and ingredients. Because of their magickal energy, citrine crystals, green candles and mint are frequently used in money spells. They are well known ingredients for attracting wealth. Beeswax candles are great if you can source them, otherwise small spell candles are easily found online.

- Cauldron/heatproof dish
- Wand/small branch from a tree
- Coloured spell candles with holders
- Tealights
- Lighter
- Essential oils, including bergamot, frankincense, patchouli
- Herbs and spices, including cinnamon, nutmeg, mint, basil, bay, sage and marigold
- Sage smudge sticks
- Incense sticks
- Crystals, including clear quartz, citrine, aventurine, amethyst and pyrite
- Tarot cards
- Crystal grid
- Money (coins and notes)
- Green and yellow ribbon

THE TIMING OF A SPELL FOR PROSPERITY

Timing is important. As a rule, prosperity spells cast on a new moon phase or on a waxing moon phase are to attract new money and abundance, whereas prosperity spells cast nearer to the full moon or on the full moon are to increase wealth you already have, as well as a attracting new prosperity and abundance into your life.

Prosperity spells can also be cast on a Thursday on a waxing moon phase as this day is ruled by the planet Jupiter, which governs business and financial gain. Prosperity spells cast on a Sunday on a waxing moon phase will incorporate the sun's energy. The sun is associated with gold and radiates success.

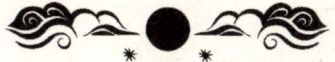

CREATING A PROSPERITY ALTAR

An altar is a great way to enhance your magickal workings as having a permanent space dedicated to wealth can help amplify your spell-casting. Set one up on a coffee table or a windowsill – or even outside – whatever feels like the right place for you.

- Having found your space, squeeze some lemon juice and mix it with water to cleanse the surface of your altar. A toxin-free cleaner works well, too.

- Add things to make your altar special and unique to you and include candles, money and crystals.

CAUTION
Never leave candles unattended. Ingredients used in this book are not intended for consumption and should not be consumed for any reason. Be aware of any ingredients you may be sensitive to and patch test on a small area. Do not use if irritation occurs. By going ahead with your spell work, you agree that this book is not responsible for any skin irritation or sensitivity while using these ingredients.

CASTING A SACRED CIRCLE

A circle creates a protective place in which to create magick. It makes a space that takes you out of the mundane world and into a protected, energized bubble, to cast spells. Here is one of many ways to cast a sacred circle to work your magick.

- Clear a space for your circle. Taking four candles, place one in the North of the circle, one in the East, one in the South and one in the West. Walking clockwise around the circle, light each candle in turn, sprinkling some salt as you walk from one candle to the next, to create a boundary for your circle.

- Facing North, point your finger or wand to the floor and say: 'Guardians of the North, element of earth, I bid you hail and welcome.' Now face East, keeping your finger or wand pointing to the floor, and say: 'Guardians of the East, element of air, I bid you hail and welcome.' Face South, keeping your finger or wand pointing to the floor, and say: 'Guardians of the South, element of fire, I bid you hail and welcome.' Face West, keeping your finger or wand pointing to the floor, and say: 'Guardians of the West, element of water, I bid you hail and welcome.'

- Face North again and point your finger or wand above your head. In a clockwise motion, cast your circle, starting above your head and bringing your finger or wand down to the right, then back up to the left to finish above your head again. You can now start your spell.

- When you have finished your spell, simply walk out of the circle to break it, effectively bringing its power to an end.

HOW TO MAKE MOON WATER

Moon water infuses a spell with an extra touch of magick. Use it in your rituals, add some to your ritual bath or drink some before casting a spell.

- Select a clean glass jar and fill it with water – spring water is ideal. Hold the jar and set positive intentions. If you intend to drink the moon water, cover the jar with a lid.

- Place the jar of outside or on a windowsill where it can be exposed to the moonlight, preferably on the night of a full moon. Allow the moonlight to penetrate the water.

- Collect the water at dawn to capture the moon's energy. Store the moon water in the fridge for up to three days.

HARNESSING THE POWER OF A FULL MOON

Before starting a spell, use your hands to create a triangle by placing the tips of your index fingers together and placing your thumb tips together. Hold your hands up to the night sky and gaze at the moon through the triangle you have made. After a few moments, close your eyes, still seeing a vision of the moon. Bring the triangle down and place it up against your solar plexus, thus harnessing the moon's energy.

the
SPELLS

CINNAMON APPLE MONEY TEA

Cast this spell of attraction on a Thursday before a full moon. The planet Jupiter governs this day. The planet of abundance, it is one of the best planets to work with for any type of money spell. Cinnamon and apples are associated with prosperity and abundance in various traditions and have been used successfully as key ingredients in money spells. Cinnamon apple tea is a wonderful blend, known for its comforting and warm flavour. You can enhance the taste by adding a little honey. This magickal blend can improve your chances of a lottery win and other games of chance. It is also a perfect spell for starting a new business or finding work.

Witchy Tip ⚷
The more you stare into the flame as you visualize your intentions, the more effective, your spell will be.

MAGICKAL CORRESPONDENCES

- Small pan
- Large mug
- Apple juice (not from concentrate)
- Cinnamon sticks
- Star anise
- Whole cloves
- Rooibos teabag
- Slices of red apple

Place a mugful of apple juice, a couple cinnamon sticks, one star anise and a pinch of cloves in the small pan and simmer for a few minutes. Add the teabag and leave to steep for a few minutes more. Serve in the mug with slices of fresh apple and a cinnamon stick. Stir the tea in a clockwise direction, infusing your intentions, and say the following magickal words three times:

Cinnamon tea,
I drink thee
To attract money.
So mote it be.

Make this tea at the start of each day to set your intentions and manifest the money you desire.

LONGER-LASTING MONEY

Cast this spell for lasting wealth on a Thursday before a full moon. Mint has long been used by witches to attract money. The word has more than one meaning and when someone makes a great deal of money, they are said to be 'minted'. That is no coincidence; coins are minted at the royal mint. In witchcraft, basil has long been associated with luck. Combining these two magickal herbs creates an easy yet very potent money attraction spell.

MAGICKAL CORRESPONDENCES

- Mint plant
- Basil plant
- Two plant pots
- Bank notes
- Cinnamon sticks
- Coins
- Citrine crystals

Place both plants on a windowsill, in pots, and water them from the bottom as watering from the top can damage the stalks. Place bank notes among the leaves near the top – they can be folded. Place cinnamon sticks, coins and citrine crystals around the pots, arranging them in your own way, while setting your intention.

Upon waking every morning, water your plants gently and say the following magickal words:

Earth to stem,
Leaf to flower,
Grow with strength,
Enhance your positive power.
On this glorious day,
Energy grows.
On this glorious day,
Abundance flows.
So mote it be.

Look after your plants daily, showing them love and care so that they grow beautifully and work their magick.

KNIGHT OF PENTACLES

Cast this spell for clearing your debts on a waning moon phase. The Knight of Pentacles tarot card represents reliability, stability and security – especially in finance. The presence of this card in a reading is highly favourable and will boost the spell's effects. Bergamot essential oil is often used in rituals for luck. Frankincense is renowned for its spiritual significance and amplifies money and protection.

MAGICKAL CORRESPONDENCES

- Incense
- Lighter
- Paper
- Green pen
- Cocktail stick
- White candle in a holder
- Bergamot or frankincense oil
- Extra-virgin olive oil
- Small dish
- Knight of Pentacles tarot card

Set your space by cleansing your area with incense. List your debts on a piece of paper, then use the cocktail stick to carve the list into the candle. Imagine your debts vanishing as you do so. Once you have done this, mix two drops of bergamot or frankincense oil with a little olive oil in the small dish and use this to anoint the candle, avoiding the wick. Light the candle, place the tarot card in front of it and still your mind as you gaze into the flame. Visualize all your debts being paid and gone. Place the piece of paper in the small dish and burn it. Now say the following magickal words:

> *Debts cleared and paid,*
> *A lesson I've learned.*
> *I banish these debts,*
> *When this candle is burned,*
> *So mote it be.*

Fill your whole body with a sense of freedom from debt and well-being while gazing deeply into the flame. Sit with this visualization and let the candle burn for another ten minutes before snuffing out the candle. Repeat the same process every night until the candle burns down completely. Each time, take the dish with the burned paper and blow and the ashes into the night sky. You'll soon see yourself cleared of debt.

DREAM DESTINATION

Cast this spell of wish fulfilment on a waxing moon, preferably on a Thursday. Do you dream of a place you would like to travel to? With this spell, there is no need to worry about how you will find the money – just allow the universe to work its magick. The world is your oyster.

MAGICKAL CORRESPONDENCES

- Large sheet of paper or cardboard
- Pen
- Photos of where you would like to go
- Holiday mementos
- Scissors
- Coins
- Glue
- Patchouli incense
- Lighter
- The World tarot card

Write your full name and date of birth anywhere on the paper or cardboard. Cut out pictures of a place you would like to go from magazines or travel brochures and glue them to the paper or cardboard. Write down words that describe your intentions, and add seashells, coins and even a toy aeroplane. Add anything else you feel drawn to for your dream holiday. Once you have glued your photos and gathered all that you need, light the incense and place the paper or cardboard on a table. Place The World tarot card on top and envision yourself journeying to the place you have chosen, then say the following enchanting words:

I call upon the energy of Fire,
the great creator of magick I desire.
I call upon Water energy,
the soothing vibrations come flow to me.
I call upon energy of Air,
come forth and make the pathway clear.
I call upon energy of Earth.
With these four elements this spell I now birth,
So mote it be.

Allow the incense to burn down and make your visualization as vivid as possible with the smells, the sights and the sounds of the place you would like to go. Your spell is cast when the incense has burned down completely.

KITCHEN WITCHERY APPLE SPELL

Cast this spell of abundance on the Sunday before a full moon. The shape and colour of a vibrant red apple symbolize prosperity and good fortune, while the sweetness of honey attracts positive energy and cinnamon amplifies the energy of the spell.

MAGICKAL CORRESPONDENCES

- Red apple
- Spring water
- Green cloth
- Honey
- Ground cinnamon
- Edible gold glitter
- Plate
- Pine cones
- Green candle in a holder
- Lighter

Wash the apple in spring water and pat it dry using the green cloth. As you dry the fruit, visualize receiving the wealth you desire. Coat the apple in honey and sprinkle with a layer of cinnamon and glitter. Place it on the plate and decorate the plate with pine cones. Light the green candle, then say the following magickal words:

Richness of this apple, which glistens like gold,
I cast this spell for wealth to unfold.
As I take a bite of this apple so sweet,
Abundance is here, my dreams are complete.
So mote it be.

Allow the candle to burn right down. As the candle is burning, cut the apple in half and eat one of half. Once the candle has burned down, take the other half of the apple and bury it in a special place with the remainder of the candle wax. Place the pine cones on top. Sprinkle any remaining cinnamon and gold glitter over what you have buried.

GARLIC WEALTH

Cast this spell of attraction on a new moon. Renowned for its spiritual strength, garlic has magickal properties for attracting wealth and abundance.

MAGICKAL CORRESPONDENCES

- Garlic cloves
- Glass jar
- Silver and copper coins

Take seven cloves of garlic and tap them, one by one, on the kitchen worktop. As you do so, say 'lucky garlic unleash your magickal power to bring me luck and good fortune'. Place the garlic in the jar, followed by several coins. Hold the jar and say the following magickal words:

With garlic's might, wealth takes flight.
A spell to embrace, with fortunes bright.
Good fortune come,
Thy will be done.
Prosperity flows to me.
So mote it be.

Keep the jar in a special spot in your home and hold it every morning for seven days while repeating the magickal words. Also keep a clove of garlic in your wallet or purse to attract wealth.

PROSPERITY GARDEN

Create this prosperity garden on a Sunday before a full moon. Mint and marigold have long been used by witches to attract money, basil is an excellent plant for luck and lavender is great for positive energy.

MAGICKAL CORRESPONDENCES

- Mint seeds or plants
- Basil seeds or plants
- Marigold seeds or plants
- Lavender seeds or plants

Simply plant the seeds or plants in a corner of your garden. Once done, raise your hands up, facing the plants, and say the following magickal words:

In this corner of fertile soil
Intentions are sown.
A prosperity garden
Tendered and carefully grown.
Seeds of wealth
Planted with gentle care.
Whispered wishes, in the open air.
So mote it be.

Repeat these words whenever you feel drawn to do so. Nurture your garden with respect and in the knowledge that it is attracting abundance to your home.

ABUNDANCE IN YOUR HOME

Cast this spell of welcome at the start of every month. Casting a cinnamon ritual on the first day of every month is associated with new beginnings and welcomes prosperity into your home. Combining the cinnamon with a little sea salt adds protection to your spell, keeping your home safe from outside energies.

MAGICKAL CORRESPONDENCES

- Doormat
- Basil oil
- Coins
- Ground cinnamon
- Sea salt

Spend some time cleaning the area around your front door and let the universe know exactly what you want as you set this intention. Lift the doormat, sprinkle the area with three drops of basil oil and place the coins in the middle. Lower the mat and place a heaped tablespoon of cinnamon and a pinch of salt in the palm of your non-dominant hand. Open your front door and blow the cinnamon and salt into the wind, repeating the following magickal words three times:

I open my heart to attract to me,
Money and prosperity.
Money come.
Money grow.
Money is here.
Money flows.
So mote it be.

Repeat the spell each first day of subsequent months until money starts to flow in as you desire.

9

MOTHER EARTH MONEY JAR

Cast this spell of attraction on a Thursday, on a waxing moon phase. The planet that governs money is Jupiter and its day is associated with Thursday, so creating a money jar on this day will attract money and success to you – whether it is to do better at work, receive a bonus or bring you more clients. Soil has the natural ability to nurture and grow.

MAGICKAL CORRESPONDENCES

- Small jar
- Soil
- Bay leaf
- Pen
- Bank note
- Dill
- Rosemary
- Allspice
- Nutmegs
- Green candle
- Lighter

Place some soil in the bottom of the jar. Write your full name on the bay leaf and place it on top of the soil, along with the bank note. Sprinkle over a pinch each of dill, rosemary and allspice and place two nutmegs on top. Visualize your intention and place the lid on the jar securely. Light the candle and use the molten wax to seal the jar all around the rim. Now say the following magickal words:

I call upon the elements all around
To bind this jar with prosperity abound.
Money flows in gracious harmony.
Growth and blessings,
So mote it be.

In order for the spell to work its magick, place the jar somewhere you will see it regularly.

10

APHRODITE GET RICH WATER SPELL

Cast this spell of wish fulfilment on a new moon while playing soft, calming music. Aphrodite is most associated with love, however her energy also represents inspiration and guidance in assisting with attracting financial gain. Combining water and coins in a cauldron is a symbolic ritual for financial abundance. Filling the cauldron with moon water symbolizes the flow of prosperity, and adding coins represents material fortune. The key is to focus your mind on positive intentions and the outcome you desire. Express gratitude for the prosperity in your life at present and this will amplify the effectiveness of your spell.

MAGICKAL CORRESPONDENCES

- Cauldron or bowl
- Moon water (see page 14)
- Cinnamon stick
- Silver coins
- Biodegradable silver glitter

Fill your cauldron or bowl up to about halfway with moon water and add the cinnamon stick, silver coins and glitter. Place your hands over the cauldron and say the following magickal words:

Aphrodite, Goddess of abundance and love,
I call out to thee.
Aphrodite, bless me with riches.
So mote it be.

Sit with your cauldron for a short while and meditate with the sound of the calming music. When you are ready, bury your coins with the cinnamon stick and pour the water on top. Repeat the spell until you have fulfilled your desires.

11

GAIN EMPLOYMENT

Cast this spell of wish fulfilment on a Sunday, on a waxing moon phase. Before casting this spell, take some time to focus on your intentions and visualize the outcome. The key is to align your actions with your intentions.

MAGICKAL CORRESPONDENCES

- Gold candle in a holder
- Honey
- Biodegradable gold glitter
- Small dish
- Lighter

Anoint the candle with honey, avoiding the wick, and working in a clockwise direction. Sprinkle some glitter on the candle. Stand the candle in the dish and light it, then say the following magickal words three times:

The sweet ladder of success,
I now start to climb.
My dream job is here,
And finally it is mine.
Wealth and happiness are here with me
As I say these words.
So mote it be.

Spend some time visualizing and after ten minutes snuff
out the candle. Repeat the spell every following Sunday
on a waxing moon until you get the job you desire.

Witchy Tip
*Always work in a clockwise (deosil) direction when
you anoint a candle, as this will attract energy to you.
Anointing a candle in an anti-clockwise (widdershins)
direction will repel or push away energy from you.*

12

A BIRTHDAY WISH

*Cast this spell on your birthday, after sunset.
Before you start, declutter your space to avoid
distractions, and create a sacred space.*

MAGICKAL CORRESPONDENCES

- White candle in a holder
  - Lighter
- Citrine crystals

Decide on the area of prosperity you want to focus
on, such as increased wealth or a career move with
a higher salary. Light the candle and place the citrine
crystals next to it. Close your eyes and take a few deep
breaths. When you are ready, visualize how you will
feel once your wishes come true. Then say the following
magickal words:

*On my special day, this spell I weave,
Prosperity and happiness may they never leave.
With candle's glow and my wish so bright.
Wealth and prosperity be mine on this special night.
So mote it be.*

Let the candle burn right down and bury any remaining wax under a special bush or plant in your garden. Thank the universe for granting your wish. Keep the citrine crystals close to you, either in your purse or wallet or next to your bed.

13

CLIMBING THE WORK LADDER

*Cast this spell of empowerment on a Thursday,
on a waxing moon phase. The spell will empower
you with the strength to stand tall and be confident
at your workplace. The results will leave you motivated
and attracting abundance as you work your way
to the very top.*

MAGICKAL CORRESPONDENCES

- Green candle in a holder
- Yellow candle in a holder
- Extra-virgin olive oil
- Ground cinnamon
- Ground nutmeg
- Dried dill
- Dried rosemary
- Dish
- Lighter
- Mirror
- Red rose

Anoint the candles with oil, avoiding the wick, and
working in a clockwise direction. Sprinkle cinnamon,
nutmeg, dill and rosemary all over each candle. Stand the
candles side by side on the dish and light them. Take the
mirror and gaze deeply into your reflection envisioning

the person you want to become within the workplace. Take a few moments to ground and reflect on yourself. Taking deep breaths, visualize and imagine who you will now become. Slowly say the following magickal words three times as you continue to gaze into the mirror.

I rise from within,
As powerful as the sun,
Confidence ignited,
Worries undone.
By ancient forces, I make this plea,
Grant me the wealth of prosperity.
So mote it be.

Once you have done this, allow the candles to burn down while meditating on the flames and holding the rose close to your heart. Take the remains of the wax and bury them in the earth, placing the rose on top.

14

MYSTICKAL MONEY DUST

*Cast this prosperity spell on a waxing moon phase,
on the Sunday before the full moon. Really focus your
intention as you create this prosperity powder.*

MAGICKAL CORRESPONDENCES

- Incense
- Lighter
- Mortar and pestle
- Sea salt
- Powdered orris root
- Ground ginger
- Cloves
- Dried basil
- Ground cinnamon
- Green or gold biodegradable powdered glitter
- Pouch

Set your space by cleansing the area with incense. Place
two tablespoons of salt, one tablespoon of orris root
and one teaspoon of ginger in the mortar. Add a sprinkle
of cloves and one teaspoon each of basil and cinnamon.
Grind to a dust, working in a clockwise motion and feeling
the energy of abundance. Sit with the bowl in the palms
of your hands to charge it with your intention, then say
the following magickal words:

A sprinkle of magick pure and divine,
Golden enchantment
As stars brightly shine,
I sprinkle and swirl this cosmic blend,
Magick money dust sparkles
Til the very end.
So mote it be.

Add a sprinkle of powdered glitter and your spell is cast. Sprinkle this magick money dust on areas in which you want positivity and prosperity to flourish or keep it in a pouch to carry with you or in your workplace.

15

TEALIGHT PROSPERITY

*Cast this spell of abundance on a new moon –
it is perfect if you have just started a new business or
want to grow your finances. The Three of Pentacles
tarot card will bring the energy of growth in abundance.
Allspice is ruled by the planet Mars, element of
fire, which is good for speeding things up and giving
your spell a fruitful kick.*

MAGICKAL CORRESPONDENCES

- White tealight
- Silver coin
- Mint oil
- Allspice
- Three of Pentacles tarot card
- Lighter
- Small citrine crystal

Take the tealight out of its tin holder and place the coin in there instead. Add two drops of mint oil and a pinch of allspice, then place the candle back in the holder and stand it on the tarot card. Light the candle, and holding the crystal, say the following magickal words:

Words of power,
Mystical law,
Abundance grows for ever and more.
Power of the tarot and elements around,
This spell is cast,
New wealth found.
So mote it be.

Allow the candle to burn while charging it with your intention – picture the desired outcome in your mind. Once the candle has burned down, bury any remaining wax in the ground and leave the crystal on top. Sit the tarot card on a windowsill. Abundance has been sparked and is on its way.

43

16

LUCKY APPLE ABUNDANCE

Cast this spell of abundance on a full moon. In prosperity spells, apples are considered a symbol of wealth and abundance. Oats symbolize growth and the sowing of seeds to reap the rewards for prosperity, ensuring a fruitful outcome in life. When an apple is sliced horizontally it reveals a pentagram shape, which is associated with luck and protection. In this spell, it is where your words of desire are placed and sealed.

MAGICKAL CORRESPONDENCES

- Incense
- Lighter
- Paper
- Pen
- Mortar and pestle
- Oats
- Red apple
- Knife
- Chilli flakes
- Peppermint leaves
- Dried basil
- String
- Cloves

Cleanse your space using a little incense before you start. Write your full name and all your wishes on a piece of paper, then roll it into a scroll. Place a handful of oats in the mortar and grind them to a powder. Slice the apple horizontally revealing the pentagram shape. Cut a hole into the core and place the paper scroll in the pentagram area so that it stands upright. Sprinkle the ground oats and some chilli flakes around the scroll, then place three peppermint leaves on top and add a sprinkle of basil. Cut a hole into the core of the second half of apple and bring the two halves together. Bind them tightly with string, then say the following magickal words:

Apple of abundance,
Moon so bright,
In your core,
Magick is in sight.
Prosperity and luck
Will ensure,
With success that's pure.
So mote it be.

Pin the cloves to the apple, close your eyes and repeat the magickal words once more while holding the apple close to your heart. Once done, take the apple and bury it under a tree in your garden.

17

ABUNDANCE BATH SALTS

Cast this spell of abundance on a full moon. This aromatic ritual provides a calming experience. Marigold symbolizes good fortune and the richness of the gold glitter will attract wealth. Focus on your specific goals while bathing and simply enjoy the sensory aspects of the salts. The overall experience will be a relaxing and mindful way to enhance your well-being and attract abundance.

MAGICKAL CORRESPONDENCES

- Epsom salts
- Himalayan salts
- Lavender oil
- Marigold petals
- Gold glitter
- Small bowl

Run your bath as normal, adding one cup each of Epsom and Himalayan salts, three drops of lavender oil and a sprinkle each of marigold petals and gold glitter. Once you are in the bath, and in a relaxed state, say the following magickal words:

Bath salts of fortune, I deeply embrace,
As I bring my intentions into this space.
Lavender whispers a scent of desire,
I shall bathe in abundance while dreams transpire.
So mote it be.

Lie in your bath and relax for some time while you manifest your thoughts, taking deep breaths and embracing your bath of abundance. When you are ready, let out your bath. Place the marigold petals in the bowl and keep them overnight. The next day, sprinkle them under a tree in your garden.

18

POWERFUL PROSPERITY

*Cast this spell of enhancement on a new moon.
The practice of burning incense dates back thousands
of years. The power of intention and the energy you
bring to a ritual plays a crucial role in its effectiveness.
Be mindful of your thoughts. Keep them positive and
pure when casting your spell.*

MAGICKAL CORRESPONDENCES

- Mortar and pestle
- Dragon's blood powder
- Pine resin
- Cloves
- Allspice
- Cauldron or heatproof dish
- Charcoal incense disc
- Lighter

Place one teaspoon of dragon's blood powder, a small handful of pine resin and a sprinkle each of cloves and allspice in the mortar and grind gently using the pestle, working in a clockwise motion. Visualize your intention of wealth and success while you mix the ingredients. Place the charcoal disc in the cauldron and light it. When it starts glowing, sprinkle one teaspoon of the incense mixture on top.

Deeply visualize your intention and say the following magickal words:

> *Incense fragrant and divine,*
> *Rising in smoke as your essence aligns.*
> *Dragon's blood a powerful allure,*
> *In sacred spaces*
> *Wealth is ensured.*
> *So mote it be.*

As the smoke ascends, sit and visualize your heart's desires. Add a little more of the incense if you wish. Once it has all burned down, take the incense ashes outside and blow them into the air.

Witchy Tip
If the charcoal gets too smoky, add some sand to calm the smoke down.

19

BAY LEAF ENCHANTMENT

Cast this spell of wish fulfilment the Sunday before a full moon. Burning bay leaves creates a pleasant atmosphere for manifesting prosperity. This spell incorporates writing on the bay leaf and releasing your intention into the universe. In astrology, bay leaves are associated with the sun, a symbol of vitality and success, which reinforces the connection between bay leaves and prosperity.

MAGICKAL CORRESPONDENCES

- Bay leaf
- Pen
- Dish
- Coffee
- Salt
- Ground cinnamon
- Green candle in a holder
- Lighter

Write down your wishes on the bay leaf – be specific. Take the dish and add half a cup of coffee and a quarter cup of salt. Sprinkle a pinch of cinnamon on top and stand the candle in the centre of the dish. Light the candle and hold your bay leaf, taking time to connect to the energy of the spell. When you are ready, add the bay leaf to the dish

and set fire to it, visualizing your wish as the leaf burns.
Once it has burned, say the following magickal words:

Bay leaf whispers
An enchanting song,
To the melody
Where dreams belong.
As the stars shine and align,
Abundance blossoms, sparkles and entwines.
So mote it be.

Allow the candle to burn down and scatter the remnants
under a tree to symbolize growth.

20

CRYSTAL GRID MONEY

Cast this spell of attraction on a new moon.
Crystals should always be cleaned and purified
before use, to remove any negative energy or
vibrations they may have absorbed.
A good way to cleanse your crystals is by
pouring spring water over them or
leaving them out under a full moon.
Doing so refreshes the crystals,
recharging them to their positive state.
The purpose of a crystal grid is to draw money
energetically to you using the power of crystals.
Pyrite is known to be a money-magnet crystal,
while citrine attracts success and prosperity.
A clear quartz crystal placed in the centre
of the grid will amplify the intentions,
creating a stronger energy field.

MAGICKAL CORRESPONDENCES

- Incense
- Lighter
- Crystal grid
- 1 clear quartz crystal
- 3 citrine crystals
- 3 pyrite crystals

Cleanse your space using a little incense before you start. Place the clear quartz in the centre of the grid and lay the other crystals around it, wherever they feel right to you. Then say the following magickal words:

Gleaming crystals with magickal embrace,
Manifest my desires in this sacred space.
Whispered words, like a soft breeze they blow,
In this enchanting ritual empowered energies now flow.
So mote it be.

Place the crystal grid in a room that feels right to you and where the crystals won't be disturbed. Repeat this spell on subsequent new moons until you reach your desired outcome.

Witchy Tip
Make sure the central crystal is larger than the ones being placed around it.

21

MAGICK TREE

Cast this spell of abundance on a Thursday, on a waxing moon phase. Symbolically, trees are associated with abundance and growth, making them meaningful representations of prosperity. The roots of a tree symbolize a strong foundation on which your wealth can grow in harmony with nature.

MAGICKAL CORRESPONDENCES

- A tree you are drawn to
  - Bay leaf
    - Pen
  - Silver coin

Stand near the tree and take a few breaths to centre yourself. Start to feel the energy of the earth beneath your feet. Visualize and put your energy into the bay leaf, loading it with your intention. Write your full name and date of birth on the bay leaf. Bury the leaf in the ground beside the tree and lay the coin on top. Place both your hands on the tree and say the following magickal words:

Beautiful tree with branches wide,
Prosperity by my side.
Leaves of fortune shining gold,
Wealth and abundance now unfold.
So mote it be.

Place your hands on the tree and thank the tree for its assistance and the energy it has shared with you. In the following weeks or months revisit the tree, reinforcing the connection between your intentions and the energy you have shared with the tree.

22

GOOD FORTUNE FAERIE

Cast this spell of abundance on a new moon. Faerie coin magick calls on the enchanting energy of faeries to attract financial wealth. Using a wand or your finger will help you direct your intention into the spells.

MAGICKAL CORRESPONDENCES

- Shiny silver coins
- Apple slices
- Berries
- Small dish
- Wand – a small branch from a tree or your finger

Find a quiet space in nature that you connect with, it could be in the woods, in a meadow or by a tree in your garden. Arrange some of the silver coins in a circle. Place the apple and berries in the dish with the remaining coins. State your wish out loud to the faeries. Then whisper the following magickal words, pointing your wand to the sky, drawing in the energy from higher realms:

Glimmering wings and laughter glows
Where faeries dance to and fro.
Grant my wish with magick near,
This spell I whisper for all to hear.
So mote it be.

Once you have cast your spell, walk away knowing the faeries have come out to play and engage in a joyous celebration in response to your magickal energy. They may even visit you in your dreams.

23

PROSPERITY OIL

Cast this spell of attraction on the Sunday before a full moon. This spell is used to attract financial abundance and positive opportunities. You can use the oil to anoint your green or gold candles for spell work. Or you can apply a small amount to coins/bank notes, and even your business cards or job application letters, to infuse them with your intentions for increased wealth. Experiment with different ways of using your prosperity oil to see what resonates best for you.

MAGICKAL CORRESPONDENCES

- Incense
- Lighter
- Small, clean, glass bottle with a lid
- Extra-virgin olive oil
- Dragon's blood oil
- Ginger oil
- Small tiger's eye or aventurine crystal
- Ground cinnamon
- Cayenne pepper
- Biodegradable gold glitter (optional)

Clear your space with some cleansing incense. Fill the bottle with olive oil, then take each of the following ingredients in turn and empower them with your intent as you add them to the bottle: two drops of dragon's blood oil, one drop of ginger oil, the crystal, a sprinkle each of cinnamon, cayenne pepper and glitter (if using). Place the lid on the bottle and give it a gentle shake. Then say the following magickal words:

Cinnamon dances a golden sway,
Inviting riches to come my way.
Anoint my journey with success and gain,
In this sweet enchantment
Prosperity now reigns.
So mote it be.

Visualize the bottle filled with vibrant golden energy and place it on your altar or in a sacred space.

ABUNDANCE POTPOURRI

Cast this spell of plenty on a Monday, on a waxing moon phase. Abundance potpourri is a delightful, fragrant mix of elements that attract prosperity and financial gain. Pine cones are symbolic of continuous growth and prosperity.

MAGICKAL CORRESPONDENCES

- Incense
- Lighter
- 4 pine cones
- Patchouli oil
- Orange oil
- Green- or gold-coloured bowl
- Dried basil
- Cinnamon sticks
- Allspice berries
- Dried orange peel
- Bay leaves
- Shiny gold coins
- Ground nutmeg

Before you start, ensure all ingredients are dry and clean and clear your space with some cleansing incense. Take the pine cones and anoint each with a drop each of patchouli and orange oil. Place the pine cones in the bowl and arrange the other natural ingredients (except the coins and nutmeg) around them in an arrangement you like. Charge the gold coins with your intentions by holding them in your hands and visualizing what wealth means to you. Add the coins to your bowl of potpourri and say the following magickal words:

In a bowl of spices, a blend so fine,
A potpourri spell for wealth that is mine.
With a touch of oil and prosperity's embrace,
Let magick work at a steady pace.
So mote it be.

Add a sprinkling of nutmeg for the final touch, then place the bowl on a table or an altar somewhere special in your home. As the potpourri scent softly airs through the days and nights in your house, the aromatic blend will bring an abundance of warmth and wishes your way.

25

WIZARDRY RITUAL

*Cast this spell of wish fulfilment on a full moon.
The Magician card in tarot reminds you that you have
the tools within you to make your dreams come true.
Using this card in a spell boosts the energies,
increasing magickal powers. Anoint your candle with
prosperity oil or carve your full name in the candle and
visualize your intention to call upon the power of
The Magician for a successful result.*

MAGICKAL CORRESPONDENCES

- Incense
- Lighter
- Cloak
- The Magician tarot card
- Green candle in a holder
- Cocktail stick (optional)
- Prosperity oil (optional, see page 58)
- Dish
- Clear quartz crystal
- Wand or branch from a tree
- Biodegradable green or gold glitter

Clear your space with some cleansing incense and put
on your magickal cloak or a special item of clothing. Lay
the tarot card on the table and either anoint the candle

or carve your name into it and stand it in the dish. Place the crystal on top of the tarot card and point your wand towards the card, candle and crystal. Close your eyes for a moment, pointing your wand, and then say the following magickal words:

> *Magickal tarot a gleaming light,*
> *Under the moon that shines so bright.*
> *With this wand enchantments blend,*
> *Prosperity is mine never to end.*
> *So mote it be.*

Repeat the words three times and sprinkle glitter over the tarot card each time you come to the end. Allow the candle to burn down, then take the remaining wax, your crystal and the sprinkled glitter and bury them into the earth in a special place. Keep The Magician tarot card on a windowsill to allow it to continue to radiate its magick, serving as reminder of your ritual.

26

A BELTANE MONEY SPELL

Cast this spell of attraction on Beltane, 1 May.

MAGICKAL CORRESPONDENCES

- Parchment paper
- Green pen
- Fresh lavender
- Spring flowers of your choice
- Green and yellow ribbons
- Green candle in a holder
- Lighter
- Cauldron or heatproof bowl
- Dried basil

Create a special place to cast this spell – outdoors or a quiet place in your home are both ideal. Write your financial wishes on a piece of paper. Collect the lavender and flowers, tie them with the ribbons and place them next to the candle. Light the candle. Place the paper in the cauldron and add a small pinch of basil. Light the paper, and say the following magickal words:

Beltane fire's warm soft glow,
A money spell I cast, let abundance flow.
Flowers in bloom and energy so pure.
Wealth and prosperity be mine for ever more.
So mote it be.

Allow the candle to burn down, then bury any remaining wax in a special place in your garden or a pot plant, along with the ashes from the cauldron. Place the flowers in a vase with the ribbons tied around the vase. When the blooms have died, pour the water away and place the flowers under a tree.

27

SUMMER SOLSTICE PROSPERITY

Cast this spell for prosperity on 21 June. Celebrate the summer solstice by harnessing the power of the sun's energy. The sun's magick is intense and will give you the strength to succeed by focusing on abundance and prosperity. Find a quiet area outside to cast this spell.

MAGICKAL CORRESPONDENCES

- Cinnamon stick
- Lighter
- White cloth
- Yellow candle in a holder
- Green candle in a holder
- Prosperity oil (see page 58) or a blended oil (1 teaspoon extra-virgin olive oil with 2 drops basil oil)
- Yellow roses or sunflowers
- Orange

Sit for a moment and quietly ground yourself by inviting the earth and the sky to connect to your heart. Cleanse your space by burning the cinnamon stick as incense. Lay the cloth and anoint your candles using the prosperity oil or the blended oil, then place the candles on your altar or a tree trunk. Light the candles. Lay the flowers around the candles and place the orange in the middle. Now say the following magickal words:

Sky so blue and golden rays,
On this summer solstice day,
Sun-kissed moments,
Birds tweet and cheer,
Prosperity flows and now is here.
So mote it be.

Stand outside and soak up the sun as the candles burn down. Meditate and visualize your wishes and desires on the summer solstice. Once the candle has burned right down and the wax has cooled, bury the remaining wax in the earth with any left-over cinnamon stick. Leave the flowers scattered around and place the orange in the middle, on top of what you have buried. Take the cloth home with you.

28

MIDSUMMER MONEY ATTRACTION

Midsummer, 21 June, is a truly magickal time to cast a money attraction spell as this is a time when the sun's energy is at its fullest. The green candle symbolizes prosperity and wealth. Mixing it with sunflower seeds, which represent growth, and chamomile, enhances the energy at this midpoint of the year. Before starting the spell, create a sacred circle (see page 13).

MAGICKAL CORRESPONDENCES

- Chamomile flowers
- Sunflower seeds
- Green candle in a holder
- Lighter
- Yellow or gold pouch

Choose a private and comfortable space and arrange the herbs, candle and pouch in a way that feels right for you. Centre yourself in your sacred circle, then imagine a golden protective circle or bubble around you. Light the candle and focus on your intention for attracting financial freedom. Feel the warmth and magickal energy radiating from the flame. Fill the pouch with the midsummer chamomile flowers and sunflower seeds. Visualize prosperity being drawn to you. Hold the pouch and say the following magickal words:

Under the midsummer moon so bright,
I cast this spell for wealth on this enchanting night.
With this candle aglow,
Money will flow.
So mote it be.

Take down your circle by visualizing it vanishing back to the powers above. Allow the candle to burn down and bury any remaining wax and herbs near sunflowers. Keep the pouch in a prominent place in your home, and first thing in the morning, hold it for a few moments to absorb its magickal energy.

29

MABON MONEY

Cast this spell of wish fulfilment on the autumn equinox. Investing money comes with a certain amount of risk and this is where casting a spell can help enormously. Spells have long been used to help with tipping the balance of fortune. Work with utter conviction that your investment will be successful. A purple candle represents spiritual power and prosperity and frankincense symbolizes spiritual connection and wealth.

MAGICKAL CORRESPONDENCES

- Purple candle in a holder
- Frankincense incense
- Lighter

Prepare a quiet place where you will not be interrupted. Hold the purple candle in your hands and visualize your investment doing well. Channel this energy into the candle. Light the incense to allow it to cleanse your space. Take a few deep breaths then light the purple candle and say the following powerful words:

Beneath the Mabon moon,
I cast this spell for investment.
With this purple candle's glow,
prosperity will flow.

Frankincense floats in the autumn air,
A scent of wealth
I declare.
So mote it be.

Allow both the incense and the candle to burn right down and bury any remaining wax or ash in the ground, in a special place in your garden or near your home.

30

WINTER SOLSTICE WREATH OF WEALTH

Cast this spell on 21 December, the winter solstice. In this spell, the scent of pine needles draws in prosperity and using shiny gold coins attracts money.

MAGICKAL CORRESPONDENCES

- Sage smudge stick
- Lighter
- Green artificial wreath
- Silver and gold balls
- Strong glue
- Pine needles
- Silver spray
- Shiny gold coins

Cleanse your space by burning the smudge stick. Decorate the wreath with the gold and silver balls, working your way around it in a clockwise direction. Spray the pine needles with a little silver spray and attach them to the wreath. (If they have pine cones attached, use these too.) Finish off by sticking the gold coins to the wreath, then and say the following magickal words:

Wreath of magick, as your branches entwine,
Cast this magick spell of mine.
As winter's night now descends,
Weave a wreath of wealth to send.
So mote it be.

Hang the wreath on your front door to welcome in winter solstice blessings. Infuse your wreath with thoughts of wealth and new beginnings with the return of the sun's light.

31

MONEY FLOWS TO ME

*Cast this spell of attraction on a new moon phase.
This cleansing shower ritual will wash away negative
energy and create an aura of sparkling abundance
energy. As the water flows over you, visualize
sparkling new energy replacing your old energy.*

MAGICKAL CORRESPONDENCES

- Bergamot or prosperity oil (see page 58)
- Green bar of soap or shower gel
- Amethyst crystal

Add two drops of oil to the floor of your shower and turn
the shower on to allow the warm water to flow over you.
Ground yourself as the water flows from your head to
your toes. Breathe in the fragrance of the aromatherapy
oil. With every breath, feel the negative energy leaving
you as you breathe out and the positive energy replacing
it as you breathe in. Visualize a golden light surrounding
you. Take the soap or shower gel and take time to cleanse
while visualizing your goals. Then say the following
magickal words:

*From my head to my toes.
Shower of abundance,
Prosperity grows.
So mote it be.*

After your shower, lie down for 10 minutes and hold the amethyst crystal in your left hand. Spend this time giving thanks and creating a pathway for the attraction of wealth. Sleep with the crystal under your pillow until your spell has come true.

32

FIRE MAGICK MONEY SPELL

Cast this spell on a Tuesday, on a waxing moon phase, to speed up any finances you are waiting on. This could relate to a pay out or money that is owed to you.

MAGICKAL CORRESPONDENCES

- Paper
- Red pen
- Small cauldron or heatproof bowl
- Epsom salts
- Chilli flakes
- Coins
- Ground cinnamon

On a piece of paper, write down the amount of money you are owed and the name of the person who owes it. Fold the paper in half. Place half a teaspoon of Epsom salts in the middle of your cauldron, followed by a tiny sprinkle of chilli flakes. Place the coins around the cauldron. Now place the paper in the cauldron and add a sprinkle of cinnamon and more chilli flakes. Light the paper and say the following magickal words:

Fire of magick, as you burn so bright,
I no longer must fuss and fight.
I rightfully claim what's owed back to me,

As I'm showered with coins.
So mote it be.

Allow the paper to burn down and visualize yourself with all that is owed to you. Once the paper has turned to ashes, blow them into the night sky.

Witchy Tip
Always practise safely when using fire in your spells and never leave a spell unattended. You will only need a small amount of each ingredient to build your fire. Have some water and sand close by in case you need to put the fire out.

33

MONEY MILK

Cast this spell on new moon phase to create a mindset of abundance. Light some candles and play soothing music to create a serene atmosphere for this bedtime drink. As you prepare it, take time to focus on your financial goals and use a special mug to enhance the positive energy. The spell uses cinnamon for success, nutmeg for luck, cardamon for prosperity and honey for sweetness.

MAGICKAL CORRESPONDENCES

- Mug
- Oat milk, or similar
- Small saucepan
- Ground nutmeg
- Ground cinnamon
- Ground cardamom
- Honey

Heat a mugful of milk in the saucepan. As it starts to boil add half a teaspoon each of nutmeg and cinnamon, and a pinch of cardamom. Pour the milk into the mug and add a teaspoon of honey, stirring clockwise as you visualize your intentions. Say the following magickal words:

Magick milk bring to me
Abundance and prosperity.
When my cup is empty,
I shall know
Money will start to flow.
So mote it be.

Drink the milk slowly and mindfully, enjoying every sip. Once you have finished, you will feel ready to have sweet dreams knowing money is on its way.

34

NEW MOON PROSPERITY

*Cast this spell of abundance on a Thursday or
a Sunday on a new moon. Thursday is associated
with the planet Jupiter, which governs abundance.
It is a favourable day for a money spell.*

MAGICKAL CORRESPONDENCES

- Green candle in a holder
- Lighter
- Bay leaf
- Green pen
- Clear quartz crystal

Find a quiet place to cast this spell. Light the candle,
then write the words 'Money come to me' on the bay
leaf. Hold the bay leaf and the crystal in your hands and
visualize financial abundance. Say the following magickal
words with utmost passion:

*Sunlit day and moonlit night,
Money flows, an amazing sight.
Abundance gathers a joyous sea,
Prosperity now belongs to me.
So mote it be.*

Once the candle has burned right down, bury any remaining candle wax in a plant pot growing mint. Keep the bay leaf that you wrote on under your pillow for one month and place the crystal in your purse or wallet, where it will attract money.

35

GOOD BONUS

Cast this spell of attraction on a Sunday close to a full moon. May this enchanting spell bewitch your path, bringing you extraordinary bonuses for your hard work's achievements.

MAGICKAL CORRESPONDENCES

- Gold candle in a holder
  - Lighter
  - Dried basil
  - Dried mint
  - Pyrite crystal

Light the candle and sprinkle a little of the herbs around the base, working in a clockwise direction to make a circle. Hold the crystal in your hands and say the following magickal words, repeating them three times:

Moon's gentle glow and luck's sweet flow,
I summon bonuses to bestow.
With herbs and crystals allure,
Fortune, bless me for ever more.
So mote it be.

As you repeat the words of the spell, visualize your desires materializing in your life, and allow the words to fill you with confidence and a magnetic aura. Allow the candle to burn down and bury the remaining wax in your garden. Keep the crystal in a special place in your home. Know that the magick is now at work. Be open to opportunities, for the universe will conspire to bring results in your favour.

36

ALL THAT GLITTERS IS GOLD

Cast this spell for success on a Sunday, on a waxing moon phase. This day is ruled by the sun, which represents vitality. It is a great day to enhance personal achievement. Gold symbolizes success and working with it will attract wealth.

MAGICKAL CORRESPONDENCES

- Extra-virgin olive oil
- Frankincense oil
- Gold candle in a holder
- Lighter
- Paper
- Green pen
- Small piece of gold jewellery (earring or ring)
- Clear quartz crystal

Combine a few drops of olive oil with a drop of frankincense oil and use this to anoint the candle, working in a clockwise direction, and avoiding the wick. Hold the candle and visualize it absorbing the energy of wealth and prosperity. Light the candle. On a piece of paper, write down exactly what you want to achieve from this spell. Place the piece of jewellery on top of the paper.

Hold the clear quartz crystal and focus on your desires –
the crystal will amplify the energy. Place the crystal next
to the candle and say the following magickal words:

> Bring riches to me, sun and moon,
> Fortunes dance a happy tune.
> Gold that glitters, fulfil my purse
> With this rhyme and verse.
> So mote it be.

Allow the candle to burn right down. Bury the piece of
paper and any remaining wax in a special place in your
garden or in the woods. Carry the crystal with you or keep
it in a special place in your home.

37

DOUBLE YOUR MONEY

*Cast this spell of abundance on a full moon on a Thursday
or a Sunday and trust it to double your money.*

MAGICKAL CORRESPONDENCES

- Green candles in holders
- Lighter
- Silver coin

Find a quiet space where the energy feels right, sit
comfortably and light the candles. Close your eyes,
take two deep breaths to calm your mind and leave all
your worries behind you. Concentrate on the goal of an
abundance of money. Hold the silver coin tightly in your
hands and say the following magickal words:

*Silver shines and glimmers bright,
My wealth grows double in sight.
With this coin, prosperity it brings.
Abundance and prosperity, let its magick begin.
So mote it be.*

Keep the coin close to you at all times, or keep it in your
purse, but do not spend it. Cast the spell again on the
next two full moons – three full moons in total – to make

it the most powerful of spells. Then stop and allow your spell to do its magick. Bury any remaining candle wax under a laurel bush in your garden or somewhere nearby.

38

BRING ME MONEY FAST

Cast this spell of attraction on a Thursday close to a full moon. Witches work with various ingredients in money spells, each carrying different energies. Included in this spell is a green candle for wealth and cinnamon for financial success. The herbs basil and mint bring abundance. Personal items, such as coins or a representation of currency, may also be incorporated. The key to this spell lies in intention, focus and ritual.

MAGICKAL CORRESPONDENCES

- Green candle in a holder
- Lighter
- Ground cinnamon
- Silver coin

Light the candle and sprinkle ground cinnamon around it, working in a clockwise direction to make a circle. Hold the silver coin in your cupped hands and say the following magickal words:

Magickal forces above and of fate,
Hear my plea, don't be late.
Bring me money fast,
I implore,
Money is plentiful for ever more.
With every word, let money flow,

Fortune and wealth, make it grow.
Lend me your powers, make me thrive,
In this financial struggle
I will survive.
So mote it be.

Allow the candle to burn right down and bury any remaining cinnamon with the wax in a forest or woodland setting. Keep the silver coin close to you, in your purse, or in a special place in your home.

REDUCE MY CREDIT CARD BALANCE

Cast this wish fulfilment spell on a Thursday, on a waning moon phase. The power of this spell lies in your commitment to being responsible with your financial choices.

MAGICKAL CORRESPONDENCES

- Paper
- Pen or pencil
- Green candle in a holder
- Lighter
- Salt
- Coin, preferably a penny
- White silk cloth or pouch

On a piece of paper, write your specific financial goals and intentions, focusing on reducing your credit card balance. Light the candle and allow it to burn while you concentrate on your credit card balance. Sprinkle a pinch of salt on the paper as a symbol of purification and commitment and place the coin on top to represent financial wealth. Fold the paper with the salt and the coin and wrap it in the cloth or pouch, signifying a fresh start. Then say the following magickal words:

Powers above and powers below,
I ask for my credit card balance to go.
One, two, three, shrink the debt away,
With this spell,
My balance will sway.
So mote it be.

Visualize small numbers on your credit card bill and watch your balance shrink with a thrill. Remember, the power of positive visualization can work wonders! Repeat this spell every time you make a payment, allowing yourself to envision your credit card balance decreasing with each spell casting. Bring a touch of magick to the process and transform it into an enjoyable ritual.

40

STOP BEING A SHOPAHOLIC

*Cast this spell of banishment on a dark moon –
this is the day before a new moon. Black candles
are used by witches to banish negativity in all its
guises. In this spell a black candle is used to
bring an end to bad spending habits. The
mirror boosts your spell and is well
established in spell-casting.*

MAGICKAL CORRESPONDENCES

- Sage smudge stick
- Lighter
- Black candle in a holder
- Mirror

Create a special place in your home and cleanse the area
using the sage smudge stick before you start casting
your spell. Light the candle, then hold the mirror and
charge it by meditating for a few minutes on the
outcome you seek. Place the mirror behind the candle,
gaze into it softly to connect with it, then say the
following magickal words:

*Impulse to control, I break the shopping spell.
I am no longer a slave, I'll spend wisely and all will be well.*

I will make my choices, my wealth shall be preserved.
Freedom from spending is well deserved.
So mote it be.

Allow the candle to burn right down and bury any
remaining wax under a tree somewhere well away
from your home.

41

STARRY NIGHT PROSPERITY

Cast this spell on the Sunday nearest to a full moon. The stars have long been connected to making wishes come true. This spell incorporates a moldavite crystal – a piece of a real star – to create a truly celestial spell. The colour of the candle symbolizes the night sky and represents the vastness of opportunities open to you.

MAGICKAL CORRESPONDENCES

- Black or blue candle in a holder
- Lighter
- Paper
- Pen
- Star-shaped items or decorations
- Moldavite crystal
- Heatproof dish

Light the candle, then write your specific prosperity goals on a piece of paper. Place the star-shaped decorations near the candle and hold the moldavite crystal in your hands. Say the following magickal words:

Under this starry night so bright,
My wealth grows with pure delight.
With rhythm's beat, I claim my feat,
Success and prosperity, are so sweet.
So mote it be.

Allow the candle to burn right down and burn the piece of paper in a heatproof dish. Take the dish outside at nighttime and blow the ashes to the stars. Keep the moldavite crystal under your pillow. Bury any remaining wax under a special tree.

42

MIDNIGHT ALLSPICE MONEY

Cast this spell for prosperity on a Thursday, on a waxing moon phase. Allspice energizes all kinds of prosperity magick. Working with it enhances the luck of a business venture and attracts prosperity in different guises.

MAGICKAL CORRESPONDENCES

- Green candle in a holder
- Lighter
- Allspice berries
- Dried mint
- Mortar and pestle
- Green pouch

Light the candle. Grind a little of the allspice berries and mint in the mortar and pestle, focusing on the intent of being wealthy as you mix the ingredients. Place a few pinches of the herbs in the pouch, visualizing abundance being drawn to you as you do so. Hold the pouch and say the following magickal words with desire:

Lord Jupiter, tonight I ask you to lend me your power.
Prosperity is mine on this magickal hour.
I gather these tools in soft candlelight,
To cast a wealth spell with allspice's might.
So mote it be.

Place the pouch where you keep your financial paperwork or in your wallet or purse. Repeat the same ritual on the next Thursday on a waxing moon phase to amplify allspice's magick.

43

GREEN CANDLE MONEY SPELL

Cast this spell for prosperity on a Thursday, on a waxing moon. In this spell, the green of the candle represents financial wealth, while pyrite, a symbol of abundance, amplifies financial energies and is used to attract prosperity. The inclusion of real money empowers the spell's purpose by connecting it to the physical realm and bay leaves carry intentions to the universe. Combined, these elements create a powerful prosperity spell.

MAGICKAL CORRESPONDENCES

- Plate
- Salt
- Green candle in a holder
- Lighter
- Silver coins
- Pyrite crystal
- High-value bank notes
- Fresh or dried bay leaves

Pour enough salt to cover the plate and melt the bottom of the candle so that you can stick it in the middle of the plate. Place the coins and the pyrite crystal wherever they feel right on the plate, then add as many notes as you like, each of them folded three times towards you. Finally, add the bay leaves. Light the candle and meditate for a few moments on the amount of money you need. When you have a clear vision, close your eyes and blow it into your cupped hands, then gently open your cupped hands over the flame and say the following magickal words with utmost passion:

Salt to cleanse, pyrite for wealth's embrace,
Bay leaves carry wishes in this sacred space.
Magickal elements with intent so clear,
Manifest abundance draw money near.
So mote it be.

Allow the candle to burn down almost to the bottom then snuff it out. Keep the pyrite crystal and coins in a special place in your home, but near the front door. Keep the notes in your purse, but do not spend them. Bury all the remaining ingredients in the earth, placing the bay leaves on top and thank the universe for its help.

44

MAGICKAL MONEY BOWL

*Cast this spell of attraction on a new moon phase.
Rice is symbolic of wealth and good fortune and citrine
is commonly used to attract prosperity and abundance.
Bay leaves, basil and cinnamon are great herbs to
attract money. Combing all these ingredients creates
a powerful spell to draw money to you.*

MAGICKAL CORRESPONDENCES

- Bay leaves
- Pen
- White rice
- Small bowl
- Dried basil
- Ground cinnamon
- Silver coins
- Citrine crystal
- Green candle in a holder
- Lighter

Write your preferred currency symbol on three bay
leaves. Half-fill the bowl with rice, then add a pinch each
of basil and cinnamon followed by a few silver coins.
Lastly, place the citrine crystal on the top. Place the green
candle next to the bowl and light it. Say the following
magickal words:

As this new moon rises, a spell to weave,
A money bowl created with secrets to conceive.
In this bowl of silver coins in a tune,
Shining like stars beneath this new moon.
So mote it be.

Allow the candle to burn down and bury any remaining
wax in your garden or a plant pot (mint or basil are ideal).
Place the money bowl in your hallway or in your living
room. It is important to interact with it on a regular basis.
I recommend at least once a week to 10 days. Give it new
life by lighting a new candle next to it. Don't allow it to
become stagnant. Thursday is a good day on which to do
this as it's governed by the planet Jupiter. Add more coins
or simply meditate near it to keep the energy flowing.

45

ANTI-DEBT SPELL

*Cast this spell on a Tuesday, on a waning moon phase.
Tuesday is governed by the planet Mars, giving this spell
almighty power. The moon's waning phase is a great
time to banish debt.*

MAGICKAL CORRESPONDENCES

- White paper
- Black pen
- Cocktail stick
- Black candle in a holder
- Lighter
- Small bowl

Write the following words on a piece of paper: 'I am free
from financial burden.' Use a cocktail stick to carve the
amount of debt that you wish to banish into the candle.
Light the candle. As you do so, focus your mind and
visualize yourself being free from debt. Envision financial
freedom and how that would feel. Burn the piece of
paper in the bowl, thereby releasing the debt by turning it
into ashes. Say the following powerful words:

Celestial powers, I ask for your aid.
Banish me from debt with this spell well made.
As I chant these words of magick,

My worries subside.
Prosperity is now
my guide.
So mote it be.

When the ashes have cooled, carry them to a local wood or a special place away from your home and blow them into the wind, thus taking them away from you.

46

SUCCESSFUL ONLINE BUSINESS

Cast this spell of wish fulfilment on a Thursday or a Sunday, on a waxing moon phase. A white candle is used in spells for purity and to ignite a spark for success. Bay leaves are perfect for attracting money to a business and clear quartz is used to amplify success.

MAGICKAL CORRESPONDENCES

- White candle in a holder
- Cinnamon incense
- Lighter
- Bay leaf
- Pen
- Heatproof dish
- Clear quartz crystal

Light both the candle and incense, then write the name of your business on the bay leaf. Burn the bay leaf in the dish. Hold the clear quartz crystal and visualize your business doing well. Bring up feelings of immense success and say the following magickal words:

In the digital realm where dreams take flight,
I cast this spell for online success, strong and bright.
It began with a picture crystal clear,
Create my business, without fear.

With content and pictures on this site,
A spellbinding content,
A digital delight.
So mote it be.

Allow the candle to burn right down and bury the remaining wax with the ashes from the bay leaf under a laurel bush or in a mint plant pot. Repeat this spell once a month for three months.

47

MONEY MAKER

Cast this spell of attraction on a new moon phase. Green candles are symbolic of money and prosperity, while bay leaves attract success and coins physically represent money. Combined in a magickal ritual, these three energies create a truly powerful spell.

MAGICKAL CORRESPONDENCES

- Green candle in a holder
- Bay leaves
- Coins of your currency
- Pen
- Lighter
- Small dish

Create a quiet and relaxed space. Place the green candle in the centre, surrounded by bay leaves and coins arranged in a circle. Write the amount of money you need on one of the bay leaves. Light the candle and hold the bay leaf firmly in your hands. Gaze at the flame and say the following words:

Under the moon's silvery gleam,
A spell to double my money, a sweet dream.
Green candle's flame, prosperity's glee,
Bay leaf and coins, manifest quickly for me.
So mote it be.

Allow the candle to burn right down. Keep the bay leaf with the amount you wrote on it in your purse or wallet. Bury any remaining wax and the other bay leaves under a cedar tree and keep the coins in a prominent place in your home. Whenever you go out, hold the coins for a moment before leaving the house, to connect to their magickal energy.

48

BUSINESS CARD SUCCESS

*Cast this spell for success on a Thursday before a
full moon. When designing your card, it is a good idea
to choose colours that symbolize wealth –
green and gold are perfect.*

MAGICKAL CORRESPONDENCES

- Green candle in a holder
- Lighter
- Your business card

Find a peaceful place in your home and light the candle.
Hold your business card in your hands and visualize the
goals you wish to achieve. Envision success, opportunities
and abundance. Say the following magickal words.

*Wealth and money, they will flow
With this powerful business card just so.
Spell-binding words all neatly sealed.
This spell is now cast,
Business success is revealed.
So mote it be.*

Let the candle burn down and bury any remaining wax in a special spot in your garden. Always keep your business card in your purse or wallet as a tangible reminder of your goals. When handing it out, do so with utter conviction that your business is successful and see it as adding power to your spell.

HOME BLESSING

Cast this spell of prosperity on a full moon. This spell has been created to attract positive energy and enhance prosperity within your home. Cinnamon is a natural ingredient for any kind of money spell as it's great for success and wealth; clear quartz crystal amplifies the energy of the spell.

MAGICKAL CORRESPONDENCES

- Himalayan salt
- Green candle in a holder
- Lighter
- Cinnamon sticks
- Clear quartz crystal

Sprinkle a pinch of Himalayan salt in each of the four corners of your home to cleanse each of those spaces. Light the candle. Place a few cinnamon sticks around your home to attract abundance and place the clear quartz crystal near your front door to attract wealth and abundance. Gaze into the candle and say the following magickal words:

In the hearth where warmth resides,
Prosperity, let it be my guide.
Candles flicker, spirits bright.

Abundance flows here, day and night.
So mote it be.

You can recast this spell once a month to keep wealth and prosperity flowing into your home.

ABUNDANCE GRATITUDE

Cast this spell of thanks on a new moon. The green candle attracts wealth and prosperity, cinnamon attracts warmth and energy and fruit is symbolic of the sweetness of life.

MAGICKAL CORRESPONDENCES

- Green candle in a holder
- Extra-virgin olive oil
- Ground cinnamon
- Bowl of fruit (apples are a good choice)
- Lighter

Rub a little oil on the candle and sprinkle it with cinnamon. Place the candle next to the bowl of fruit and light it. Say the following magickal words:

By the powers above and below,
I ask the blessings of abundance to show.
Grateful for the happiness that life bestows,
I manifest wealth and prosperity, and watch it grow.
So mote it be.

Let the candle burn right down and bury any remaining wax and the fruit in a forest or woodland.

spell
NOTES

SPELL NOTES

Many witches find it helpful to make notes of their spell–casting, and I recommend recording the details while they are fresh in your mind. It's a useful method to hone your craft by noting the intentions, thoughts, feelings and effects that arise during the process.

Here are a few ideas for details to write down:

- Date/time
- Moon phase
- Weather
- Name of spell and page number
- Intention of the spell
- How you felt before, during and after casting the spell
- Any other notes about what happened around the casting of the spell

The following pages are your sacred space to record your rituals for reflection.

_____

_____

_____

_____

_____

_____

SPELL NOTES

SPELL NOTES

SPELL NOTES

SPELL NOTES

SPELL NOTES

SPELL NOTES

SPELL NOTES

SPELL NOTES

INDEX

RESOURCES

ACKNOWLEDGEMENTS

INDEX

RESOURCES

Starchild
7 High Street
Glastonbury
Somerset
BA6 9DP
www.starchild.co.uk
For herbs, oils, incense and candles

The Goddess and Green Man
17 High Street
Glastonbury
Somerset
BA6 9DP
www.goddessandgreenman.co.uk
For moon calendars, moon and planetary aspect diaries,
candle holders and altar tools

The Crystal Healer
Suite F1, Unit 1,
The Verulam Estate
224 London Road
St Albans
Hertfordshire
AL1 1JB
www.thecrystalhealer.co.uk
For crystals that owner Philip Permutt sources
himself from all around the world

ABOUT THE AUTHOR

Dee Johnson is a third-degree Wiccan High Priestess and expert spell-crafter. She has been teaching Witchcraft and Wicca for many years, helping others who are drawn to this ancient craft.

@themodern.witch
www.themodernwitch.co.uk

ACKNOWLEDGEMENTS

Thank you to Christopher Falconer, now in spirit, for his knowledge and for inviting me to join the Ashridge Coven. Also to my then coven sisters Christine and Linda and to my then coven brother Paul. They all gave me a tremendous amount of knowledge and time and we shared many meetings in Wendover and had such magickal and mystickal times. I feel blessed to have known them as part of my witch world. In more recent times, thank you to all my coven friends; we have shared so many magickal times.

I believe what is meant for you will never pass you by.